Film Actors
Volume 13
Buster Keaton

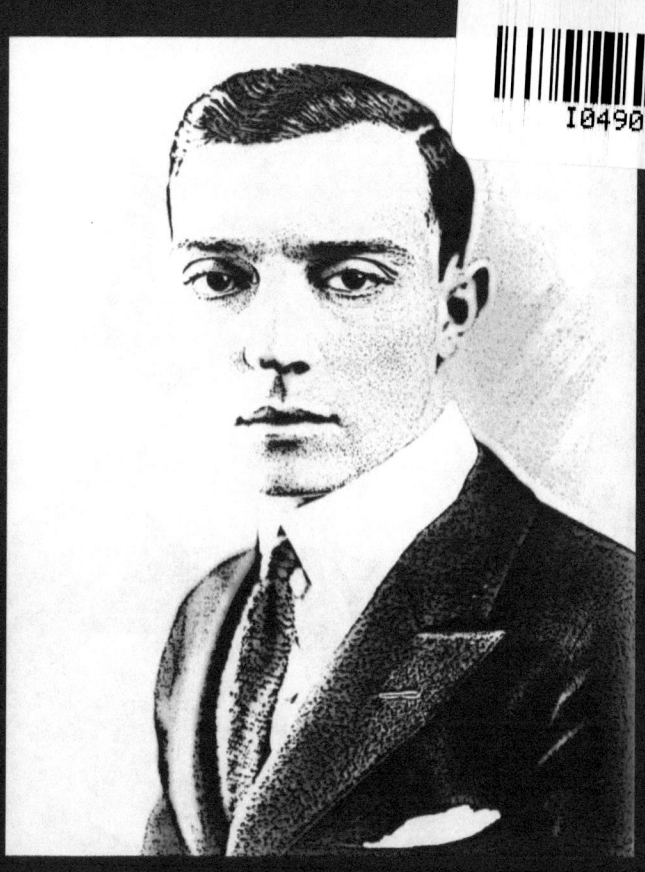

ISBN-13 : 978-1492816652
ISBN-10 : 1492816655

Dtp and graphic design
Iacob Adrian

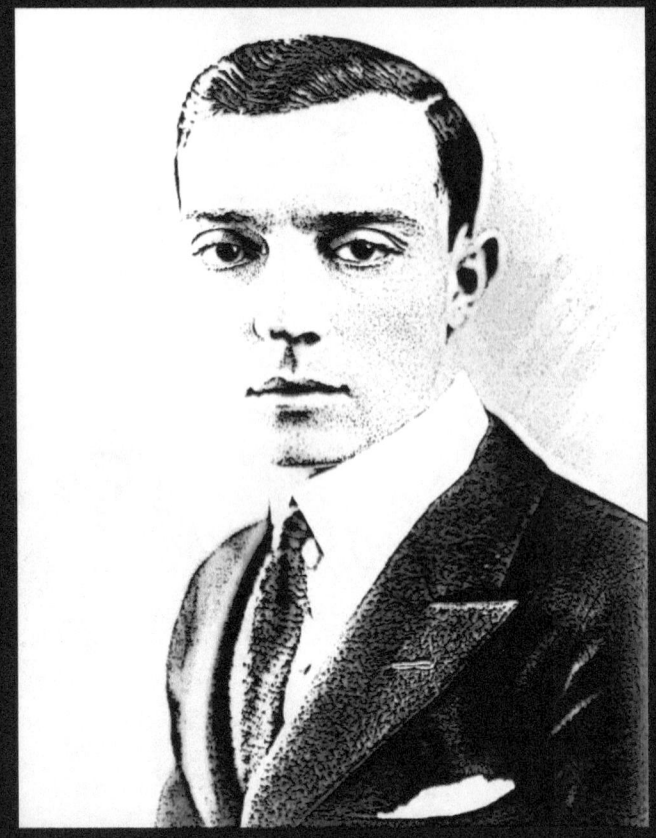

Author statement

The actors and actresses are the the bricks .

The cast and crew are the plaster .

They stand on the foundation created by producers and writers and directors .

All these people creates the great palace of the art of film .

Iacob Adrian - 2013

This documentary study book series are using, combined in various proportions, elements from the following categories, forms and subsets :

- documentary

- documentary photography

- feature

- journalism

- arts journalism

- visual journalism

- photojournalism

- celebrity photography

in order to :

- employ material as the object of cultural critique ,

- quote to illustrate an argument or point ,

- use material in historical sequence,

providing independent opinion,

using photos, press articles, advertisements, opinions of fans etc. ...

This series of documentary study books is the starting point,

in order to preserve, with effort,

the history and the film history ...

The concept will be revised and developed in years ...

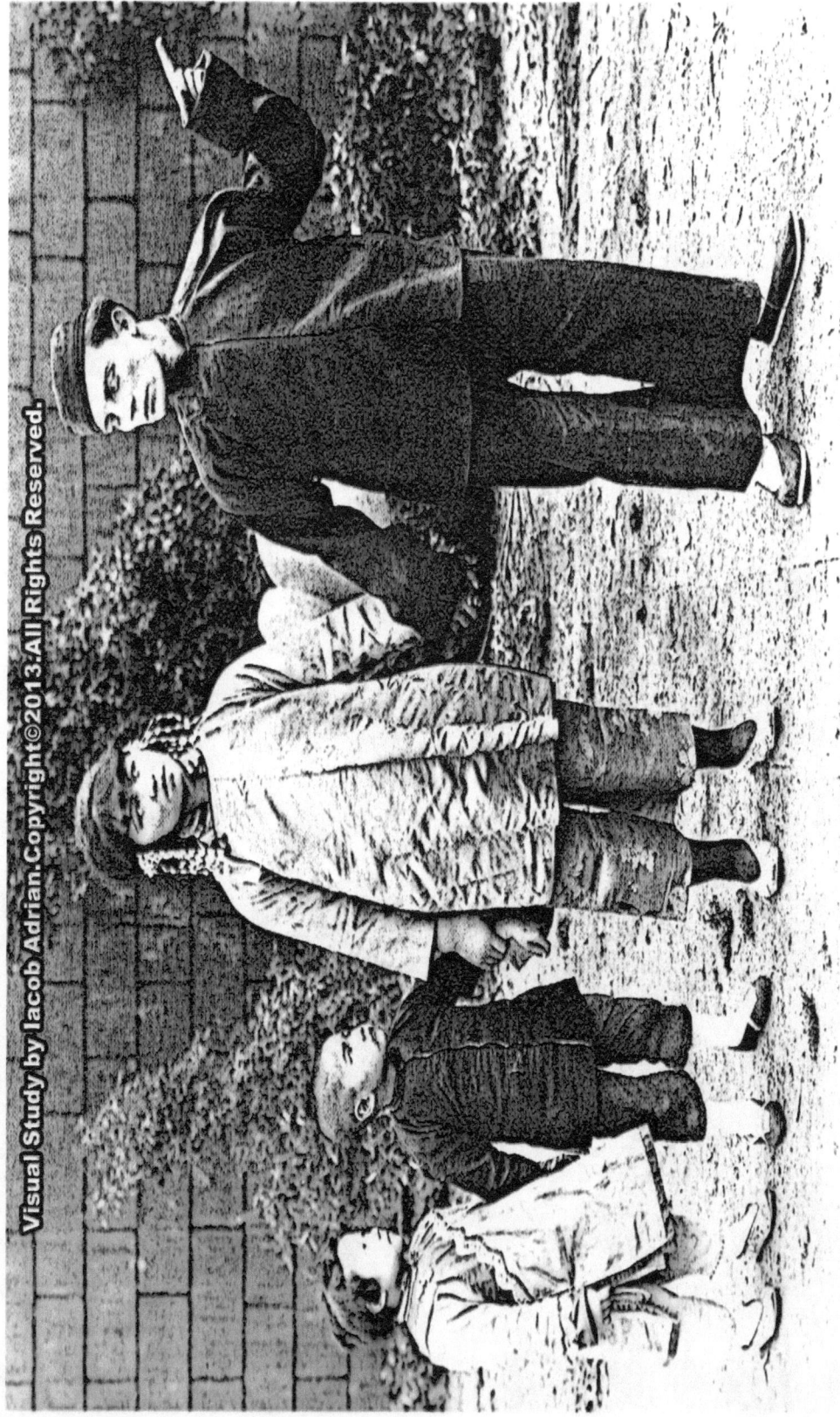

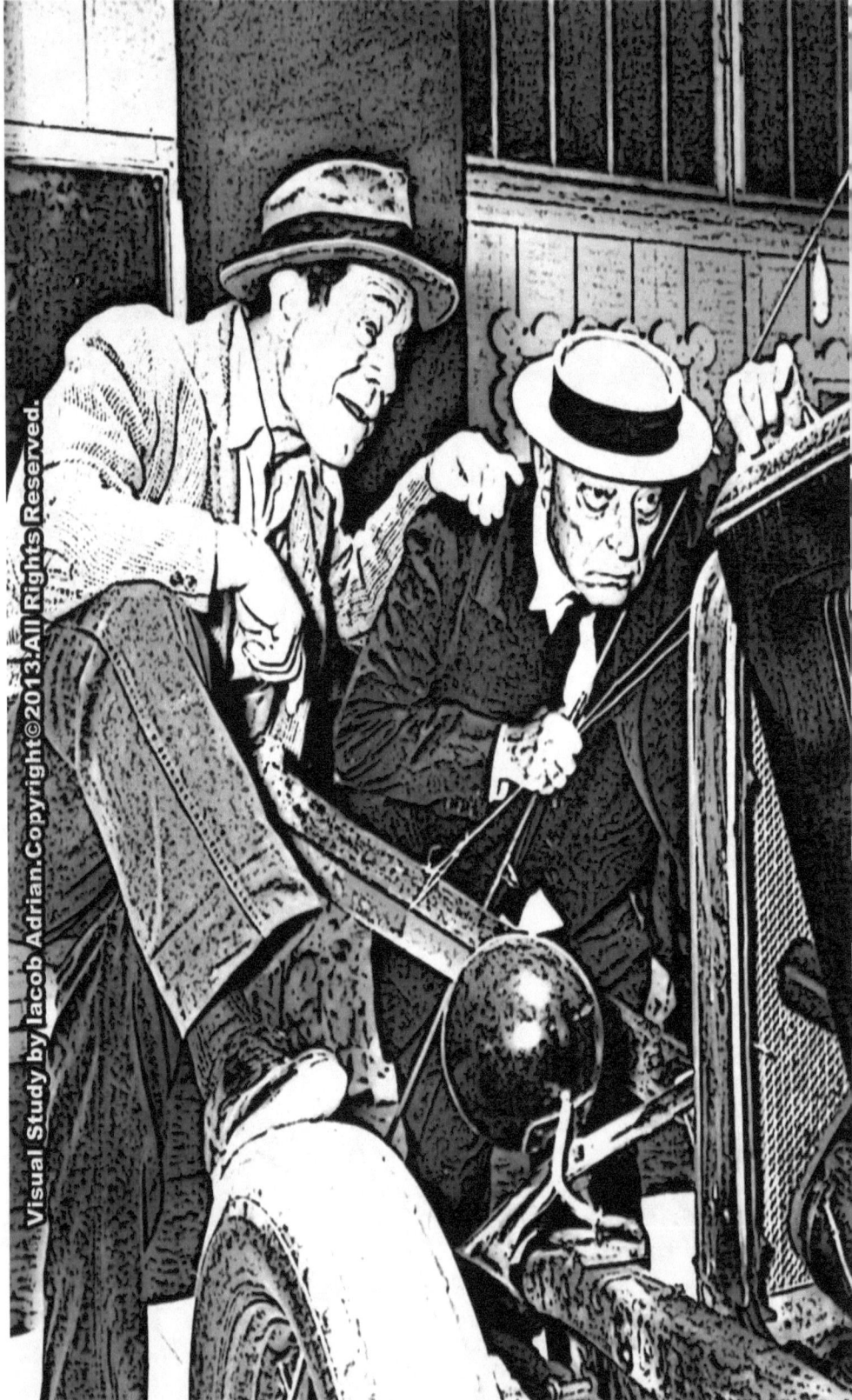

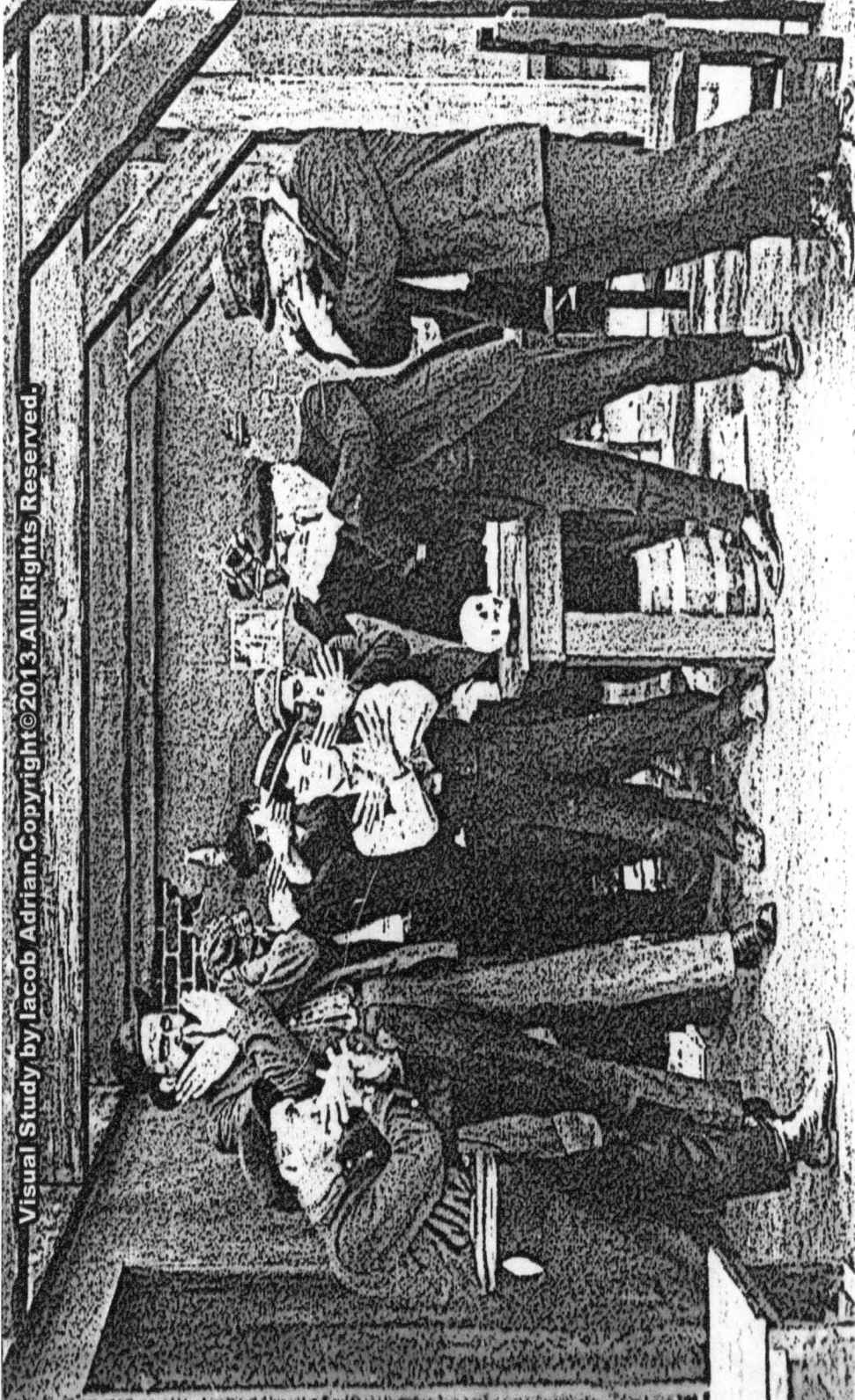

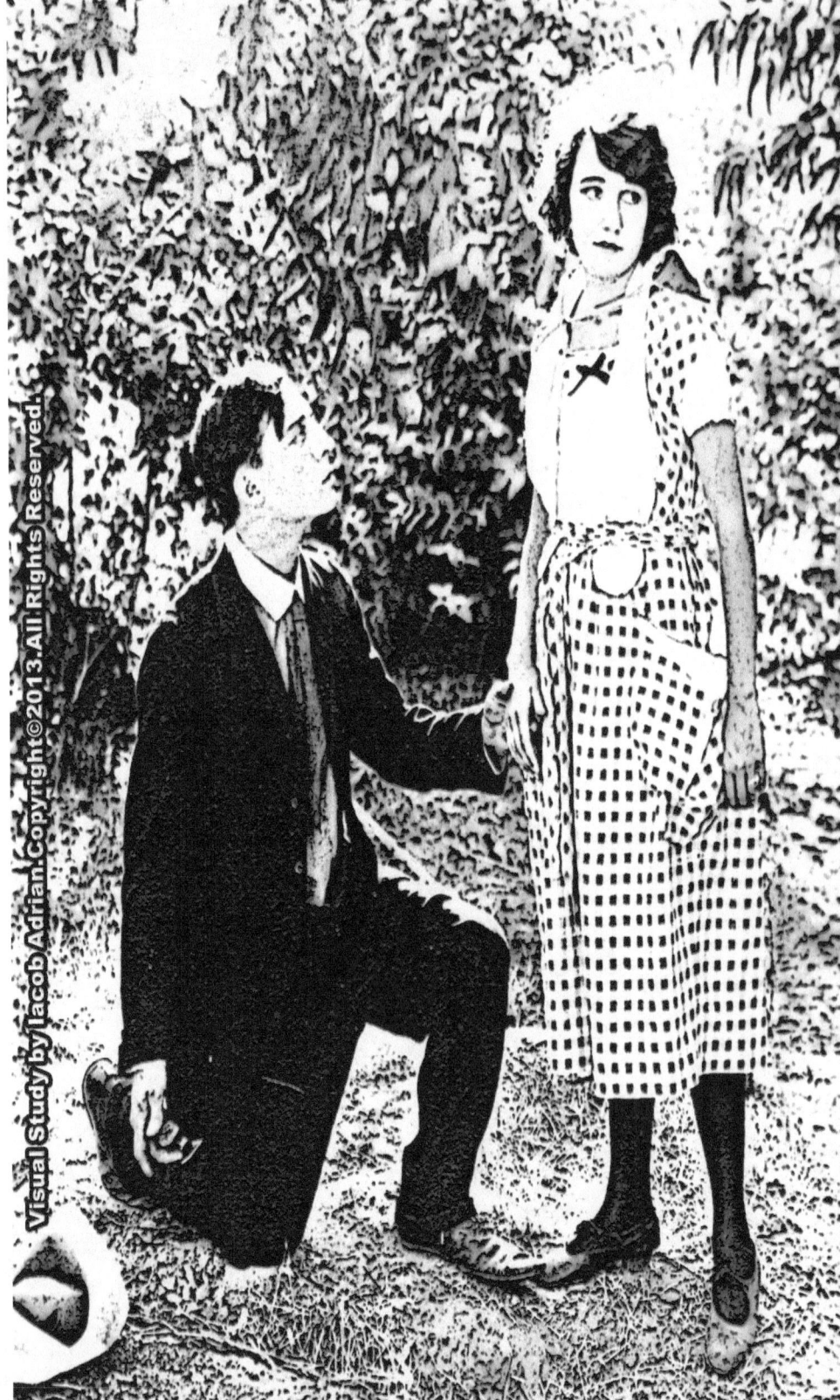

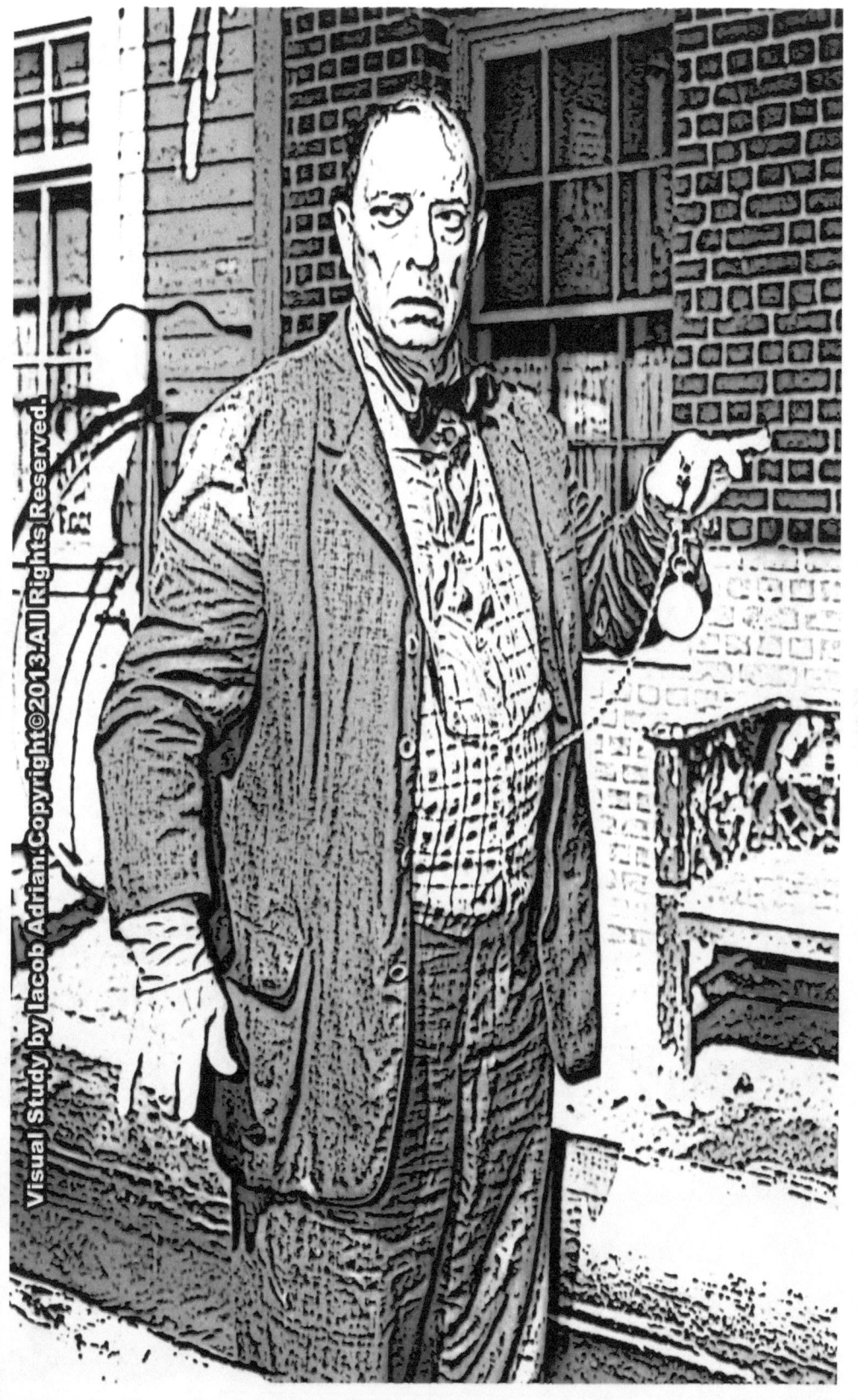

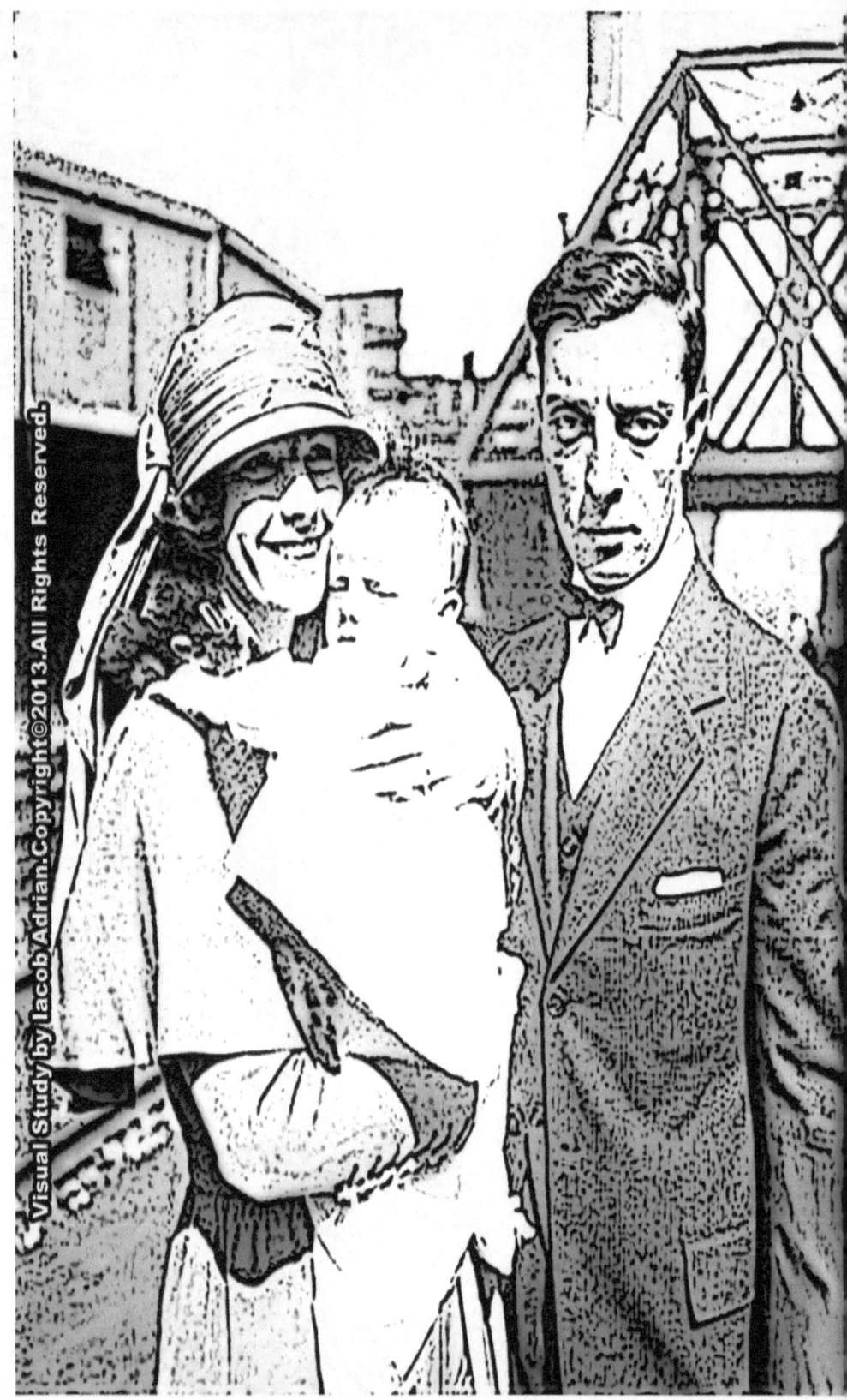

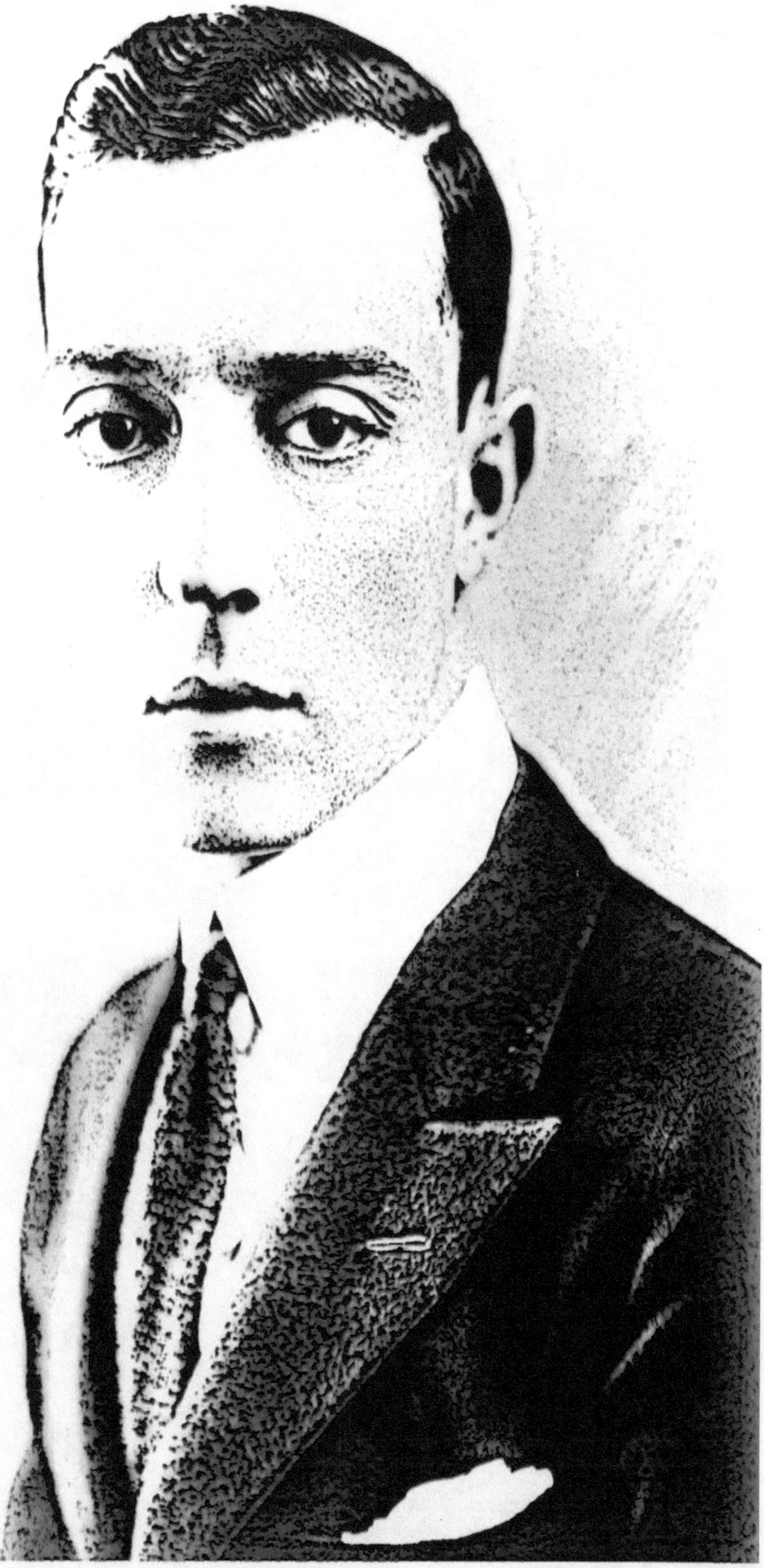

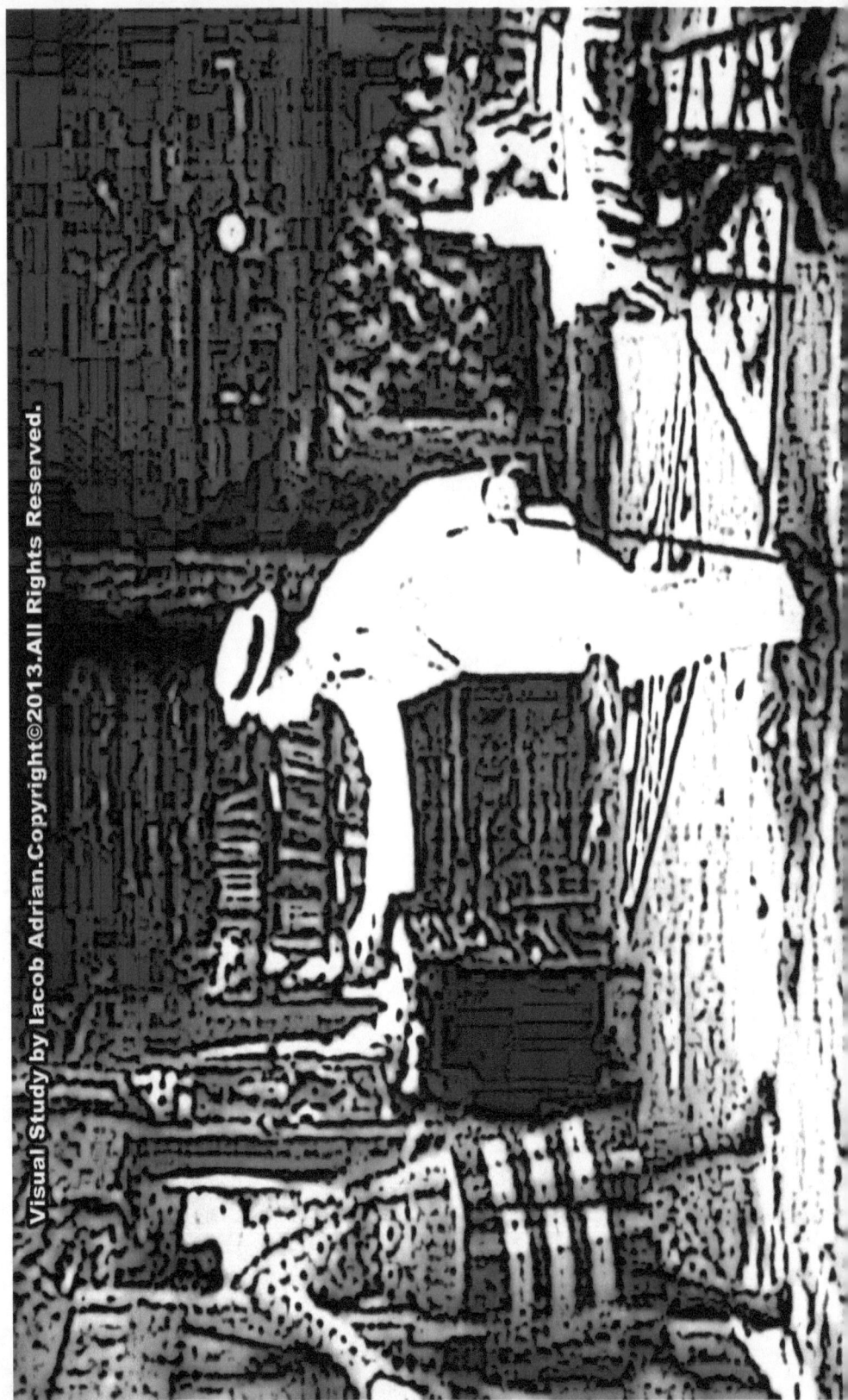

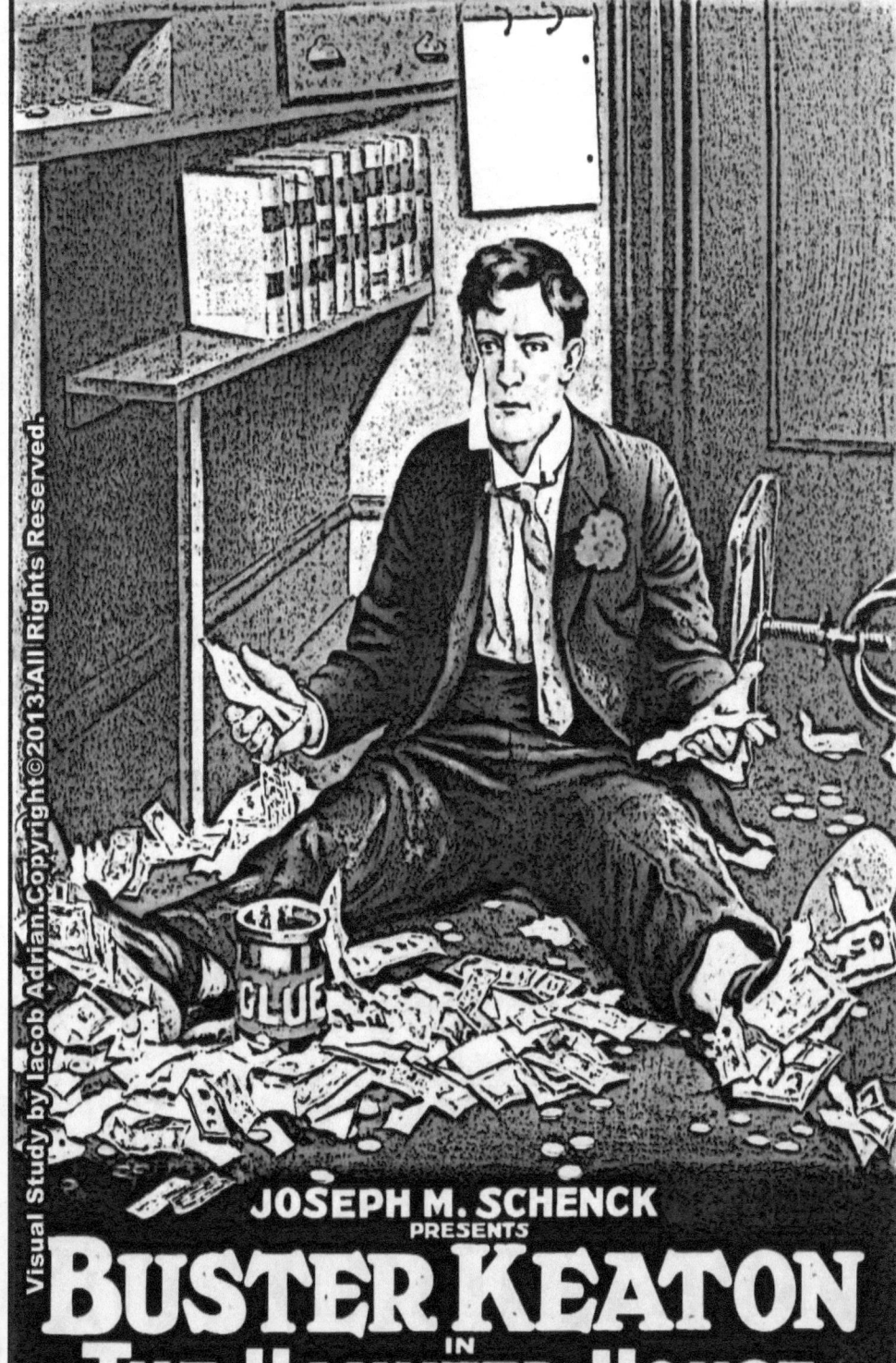

JOSEPH M. SCHENCK

PRESENTS

BUSTER KEATON

IN

THE HAUNTED HOUSE

Written and Directed By
BUSTER KEATON & EDDIE CLINE

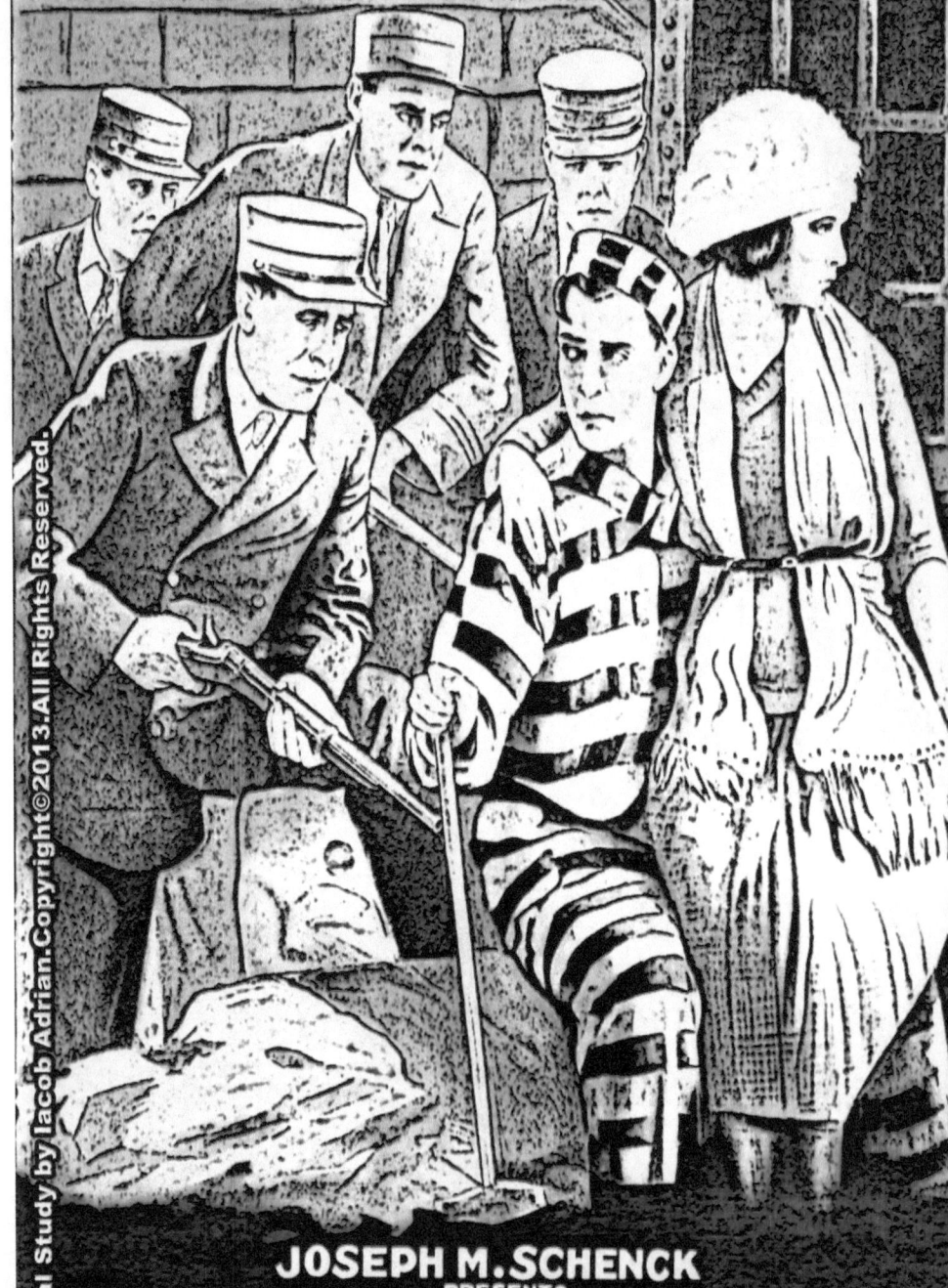

JOSEPH M. SCHENCK

PRESENTS

BUSTER KEATON

IN

CONVICT 13

Written and Directed by
BUSTER KEATON & EDDIE CLINE

COPS!
— a roar from
the riot squad!

ITS
**BUSTER'S
KEATONS**
latest!

It's handcuffed all the laughs.

Presented by Joseph M.Schenck

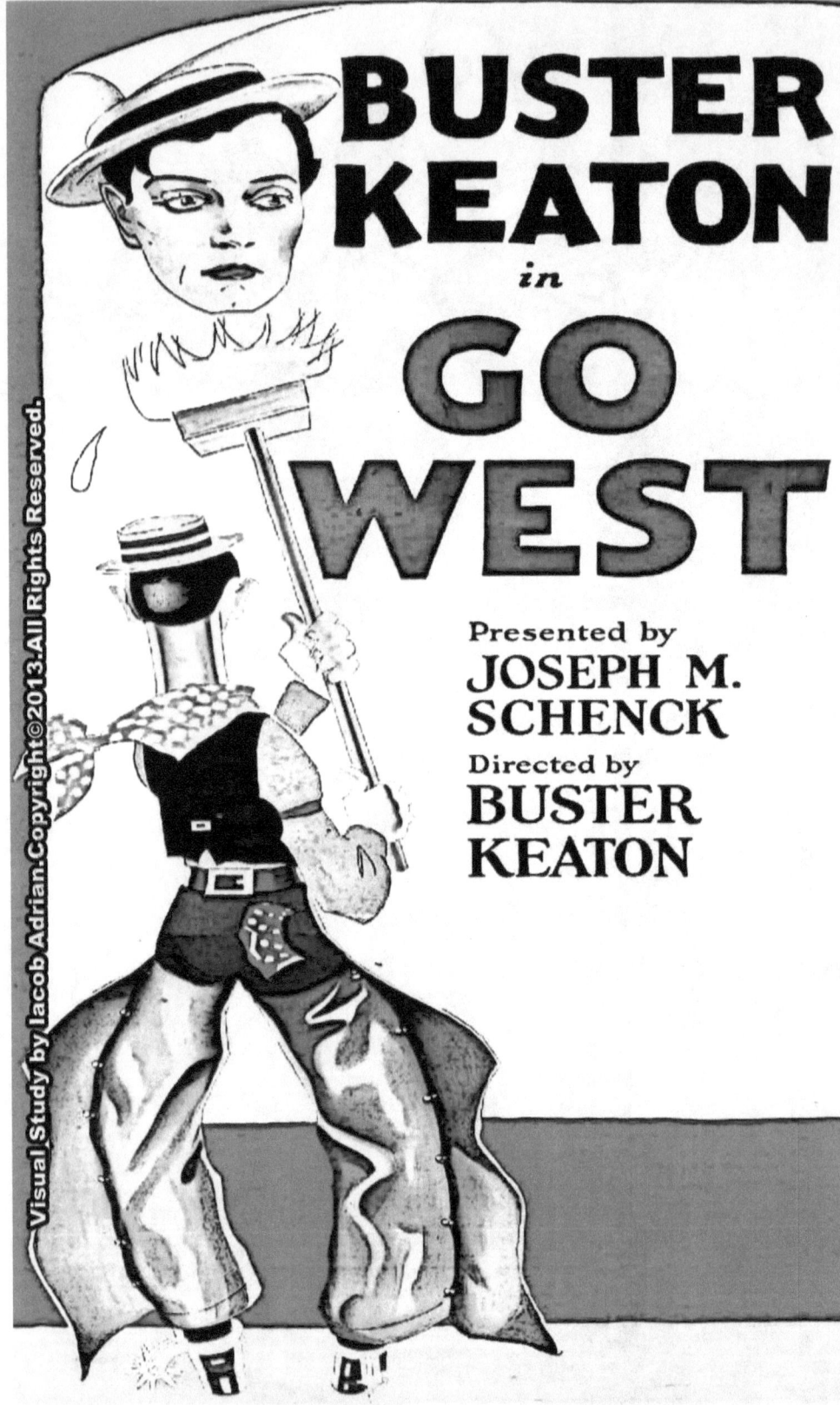

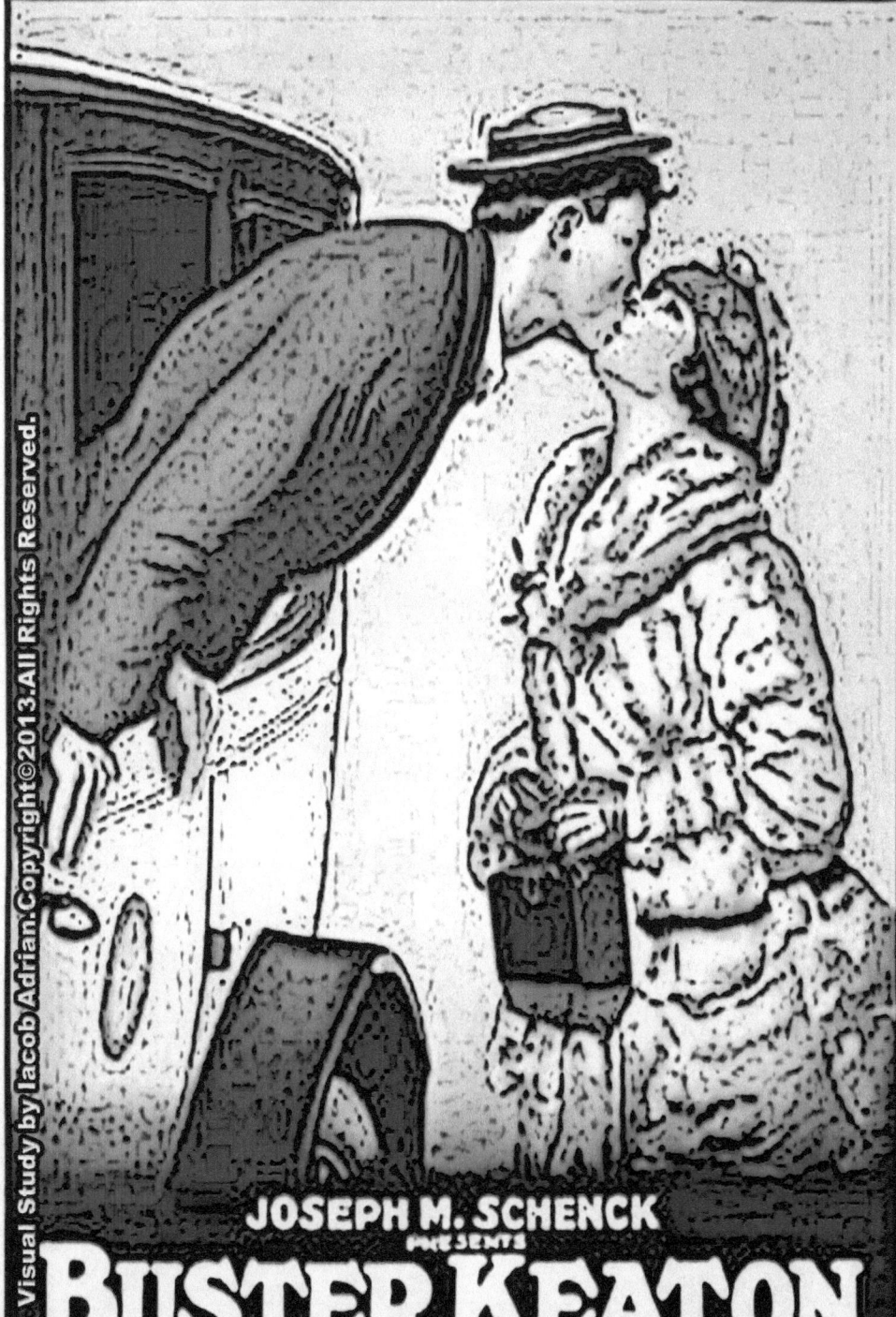

JOSEPH M. SCHENCK

PRESENTS

BUSTER KEATON
IN
THE GOAT

Written and Directed By
BUSTER KEATON & EDDIE CLINE

BUSTER KEATON

1895 ✦ 1966

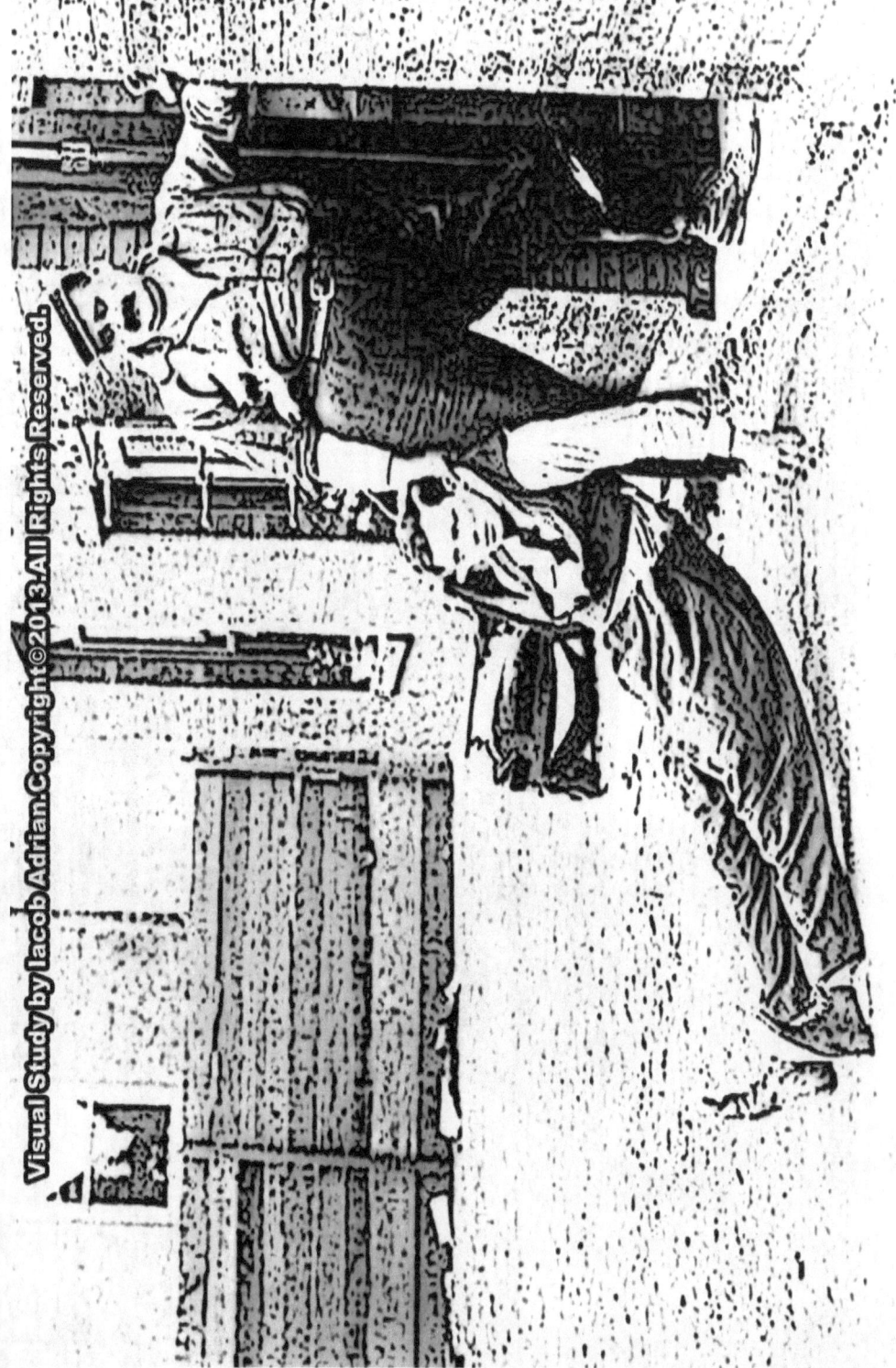

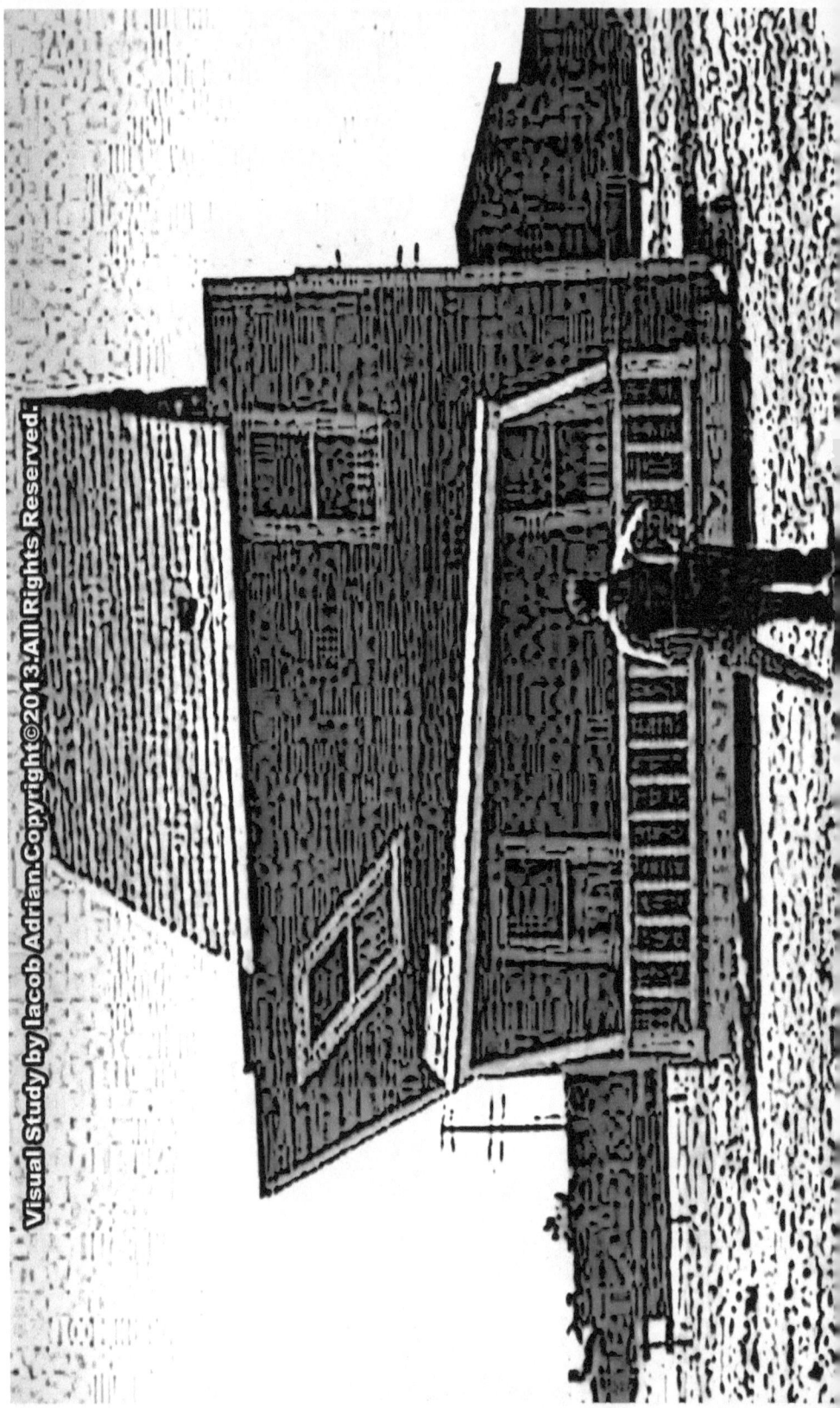

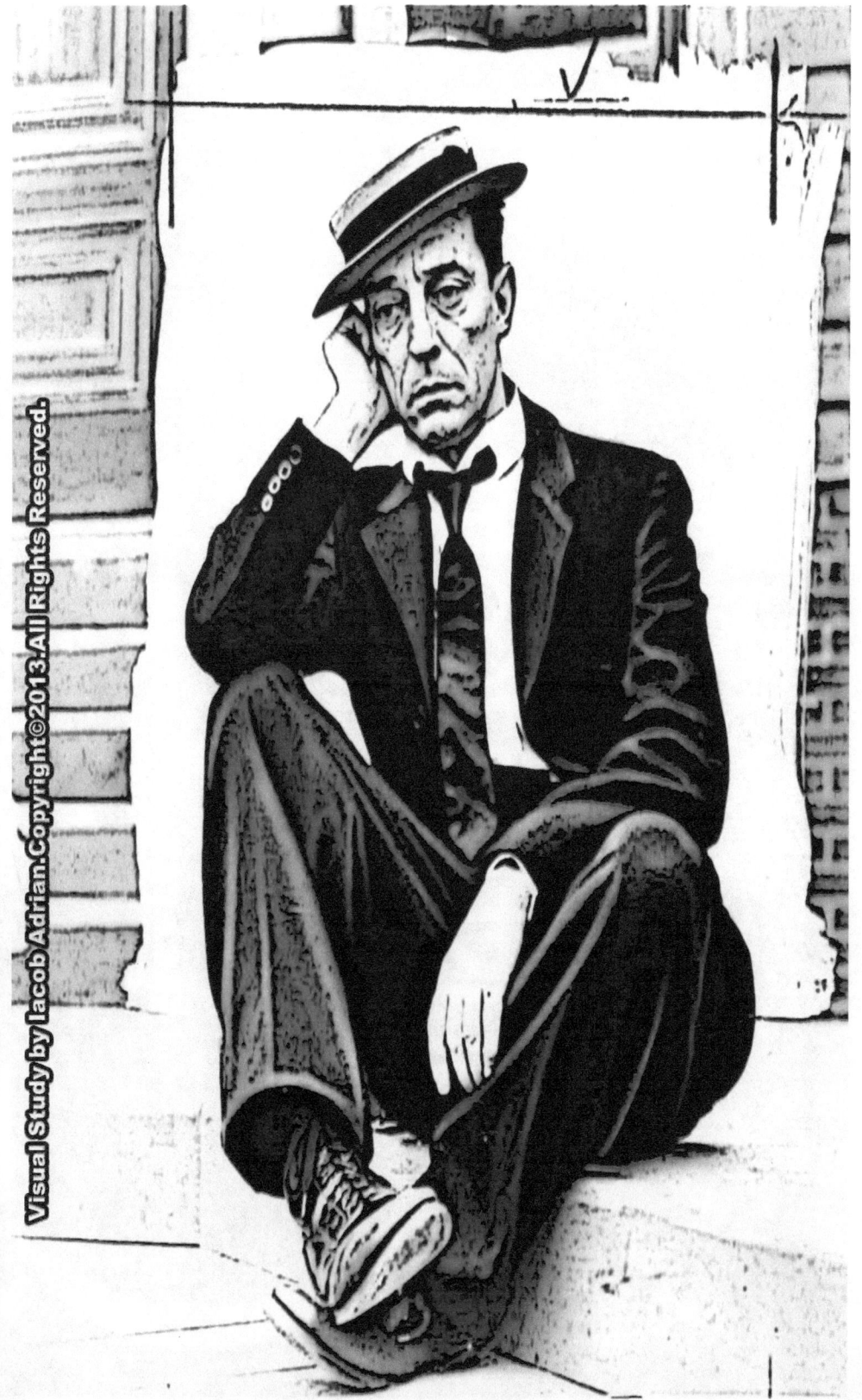

Joseph M.Schenck Presents

Buster Keaton
in
ONE WEEK

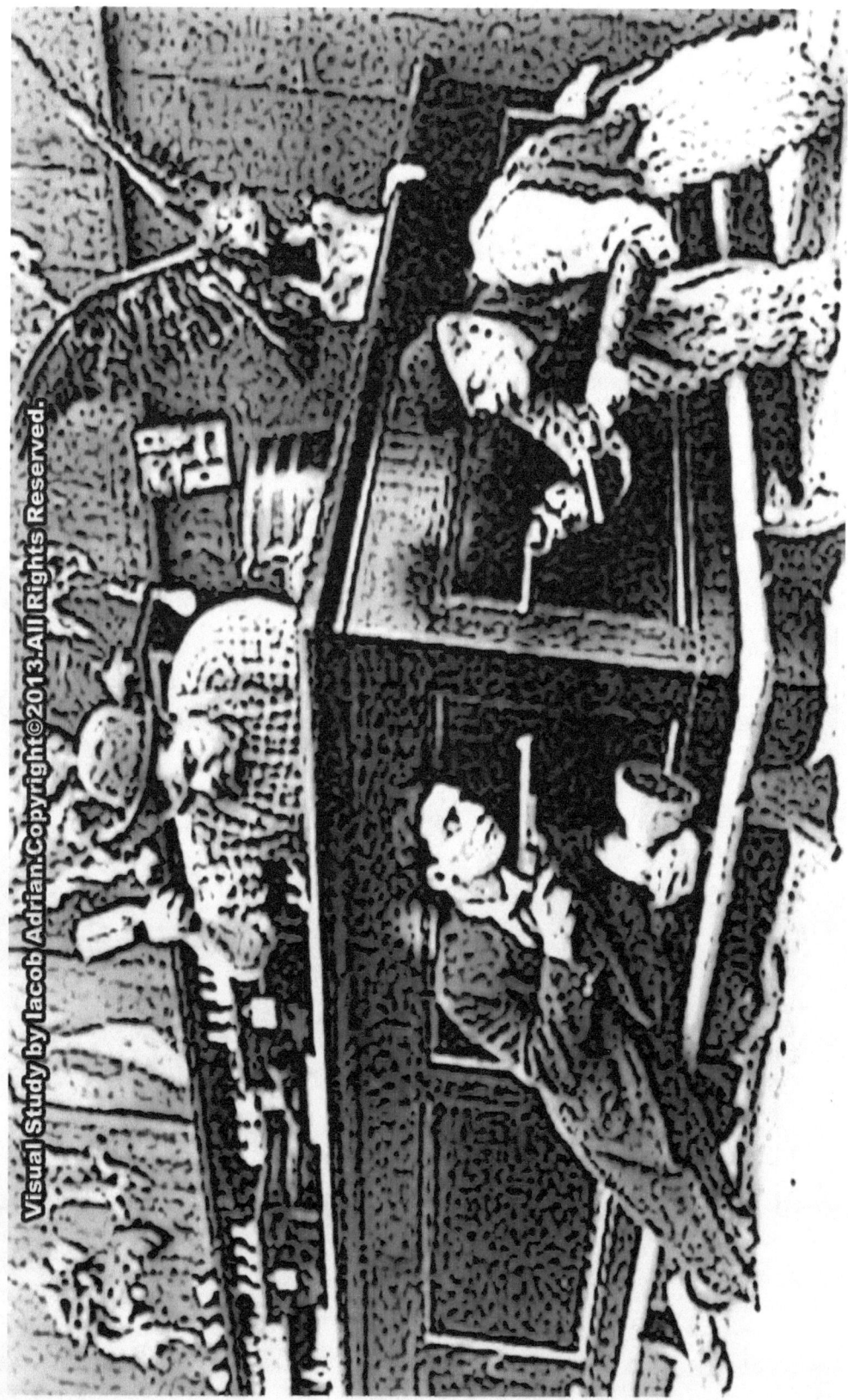

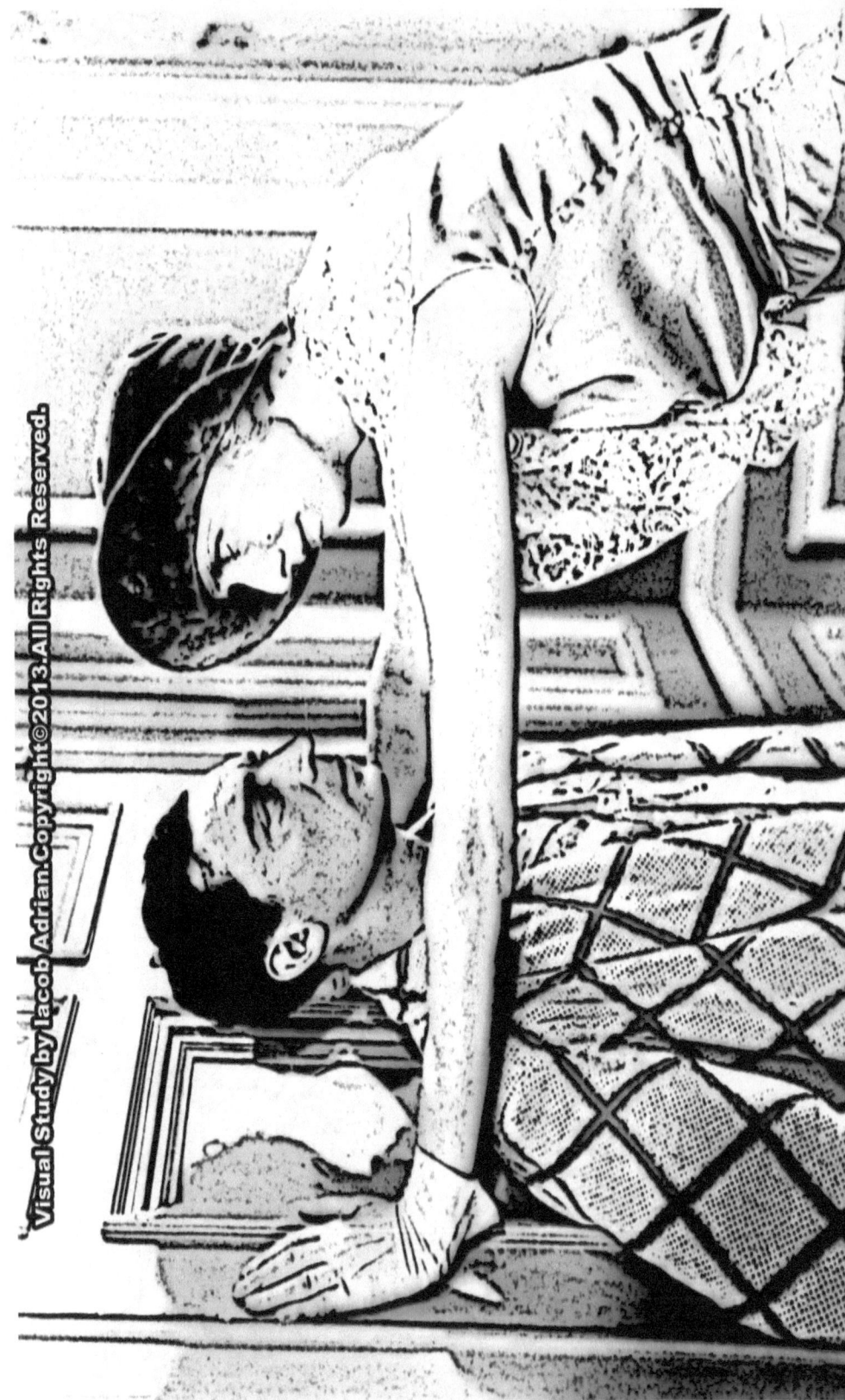

BUSTER KEATON *in*

The NAVIGATOR

He was perfectly at home in the water

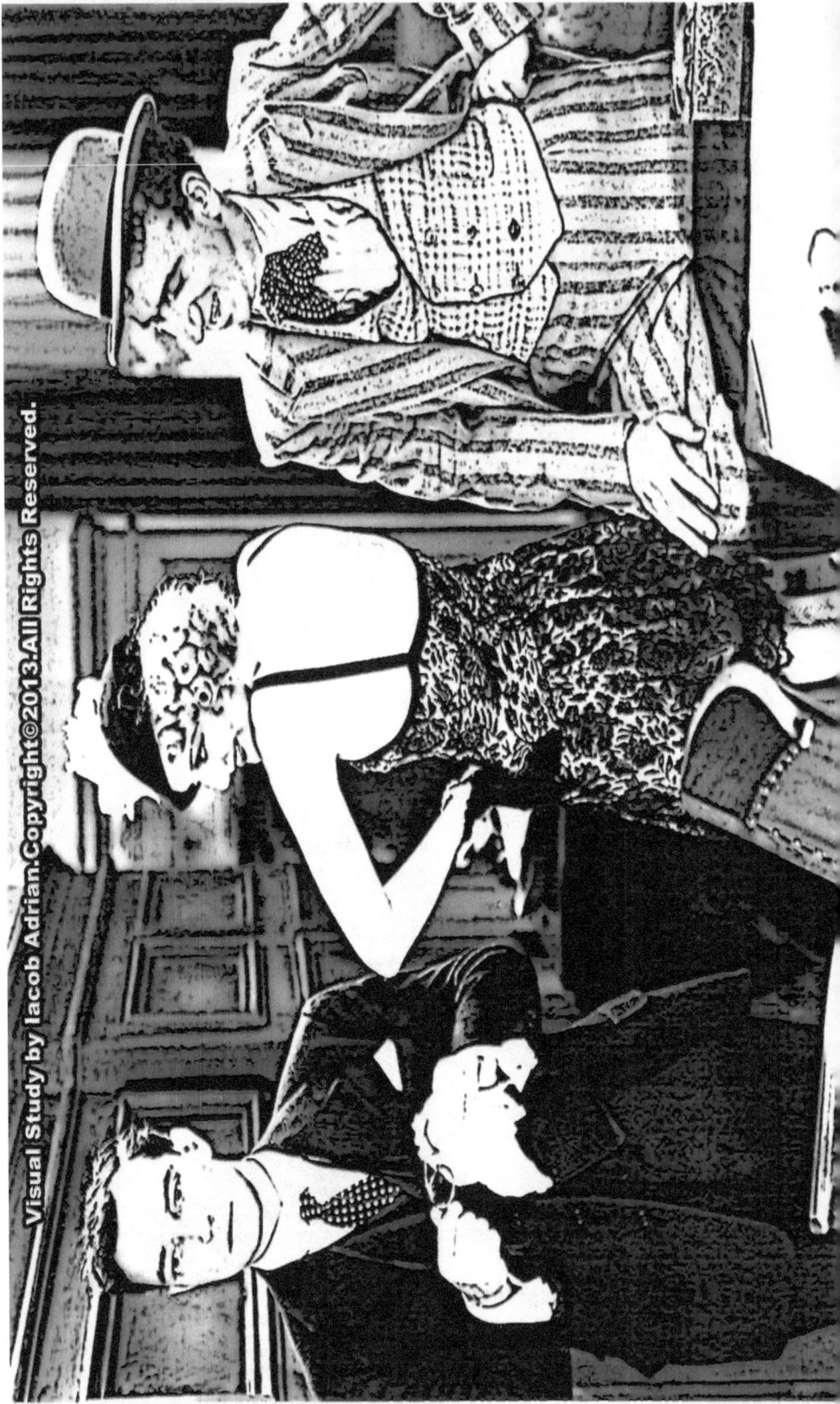

DET ELEKTRISKA HUSET

BUSTER KEATON

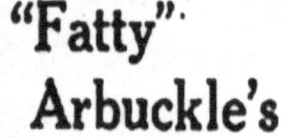

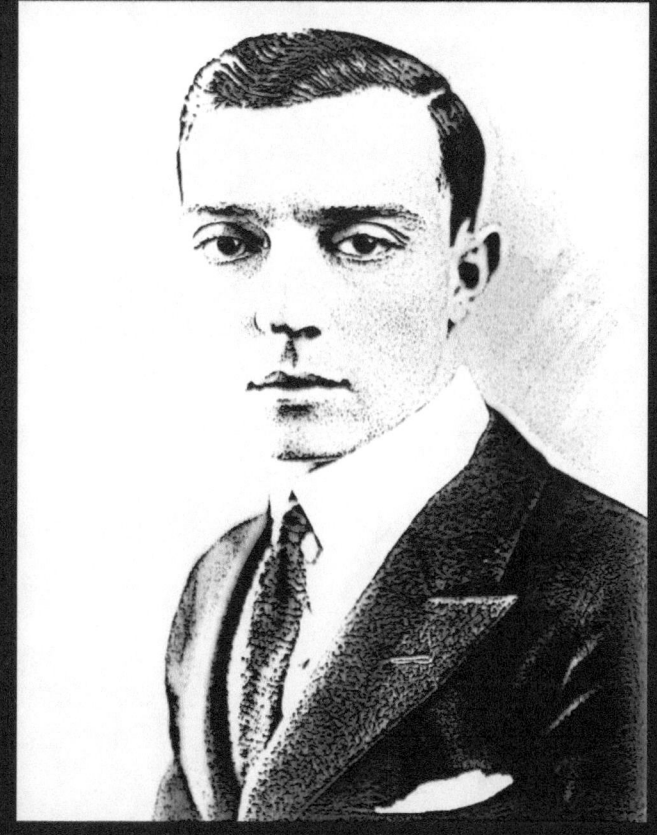